A+
books

Camels Are Awesome!

by Allan Morey

Consultant: Jackie Gai, DVM
Wildlife Veterinarian
Vacaville, California

CAPSTONE PRESS
a capstone imprint

A+ Books are published by Capstone Press,
1710 Roe Crest Drive, North Mankato, Minnesota 56003
www.capstonepub.com

Library of Congress Cataloging-in-Publication Data
Morey, Allan, author.
Camels are awesome! / by Allan Morey.
pages cm. — (A+ books. Awesome Asian animals)
Summary: "Introduces young readers to camels, including physical characteristics, behavior, habitat, diet,
and life cycle"— Provided by publisher.
Audience: Ages 4–8.
Audience: K to grade 3.
Includes bibliographical references and index.
ISBN 978-1-4914-3904-3 (library binding)
ISBN 978-1-4914-3923-4 (paperback)
ISBN 978-1-4914-3933-3 (eBook PDF)
1. Camels—Juvenile literature. I. Title.
QL737.U54M67 2016
599.63'62—dc23   2014045602

Editorial Credits
Michelle Hasselius, editor; Peggie Carley, designer; Tracy Cummins, media researcher;
Morgan Walters, production specialist

Photo Credits
Alamy: Vic Pigula, 23; AP Images: Press Association, 22; Capstone Press: 11; Corbis: Tuul & Bruno Morandi,
25; iStockphoto: 49pauly, 19, Mordolff, 24; Shutterstock: aleksandr hunta, 11 Top, 14, Barbara Barbour, 7, Basti
Hansen, 10, Be Good, Cover Back, 1, 6, 30, David Aleksandrowicz, 16, eAlisa, 8 Top, Eric Isselee, Cover Middle
Left, Cover Top, Gustav, 13, 32, happystock, 28, John Carnemolla, 17, Jorge Felix Costa, 27, Mariia Savoskula,
12 Left, 4, 5, 20, murengstockphoto, 12 Right, 15, Nurlan Kalchinov, 8 Bottom, photowind, 18 Top, Rigamondis,
Design Element, smeola, Cover Bottom, Stephen Meese, 18 Bottom, Wolfgang Zwanzger, 9, Zazaa Mongolia, 29;
SuperStock: biosphoto, 21; Thinkstock: DanielPrudek, 26

Note to Parents, Teachers, and Librarians
This Awesome Asian Animals book uses full color photographs and a nonfiction format to introduce
the concept of camels. *Camels Are Awesome!* is designed to be read aloud to a pre-reader or to be read
independently by an early reader. Photographs help listeners and early readers understand the text
and concepts discussed. The book encourages further learning by including the following sections:
Table of Contents, Glossary, Read More, Internet Sites, Critical Thinking Using the Common Core,
and Index. Early readers may need assistance using these features.

Printed in China.
042015   008864WMF15

Table of Contents

Amazing Camels

Camels are known for the humps on their backs. But did you know a camel's hump is just a lump of fat? The fat helps camels travel long distances without eating. A camel's hump is just one feature that makes this animal amazing.

A camel's hump acts as a snack it carries on its back. The hump stores fat, which can be turned into energy. When a camel's hump looks large and plump, it is full. The camel is well fed.

When a camel's hump is small
or flat, it doesn't have much fat. The
camel needs more food and water.

One Hump or Two

   There are two types of camels. You can tell them apart by their humps. Dromedary camels have one hump. Bactrian camels have two.

dromedary camel

Bactrian camel

Camels have small heads for their size. They also have long legs and necks. Camels look somewhat like alpacas and llamas. That's because they are part of the same animal group.

For thousands of years, people have used camels to cross deserts. Millions of dromedary camels live in northern Africa and the Arabian Peninsula. Most camels are tame. But small herds of wild Bactrian camels roam the Gobi desert in Asia.

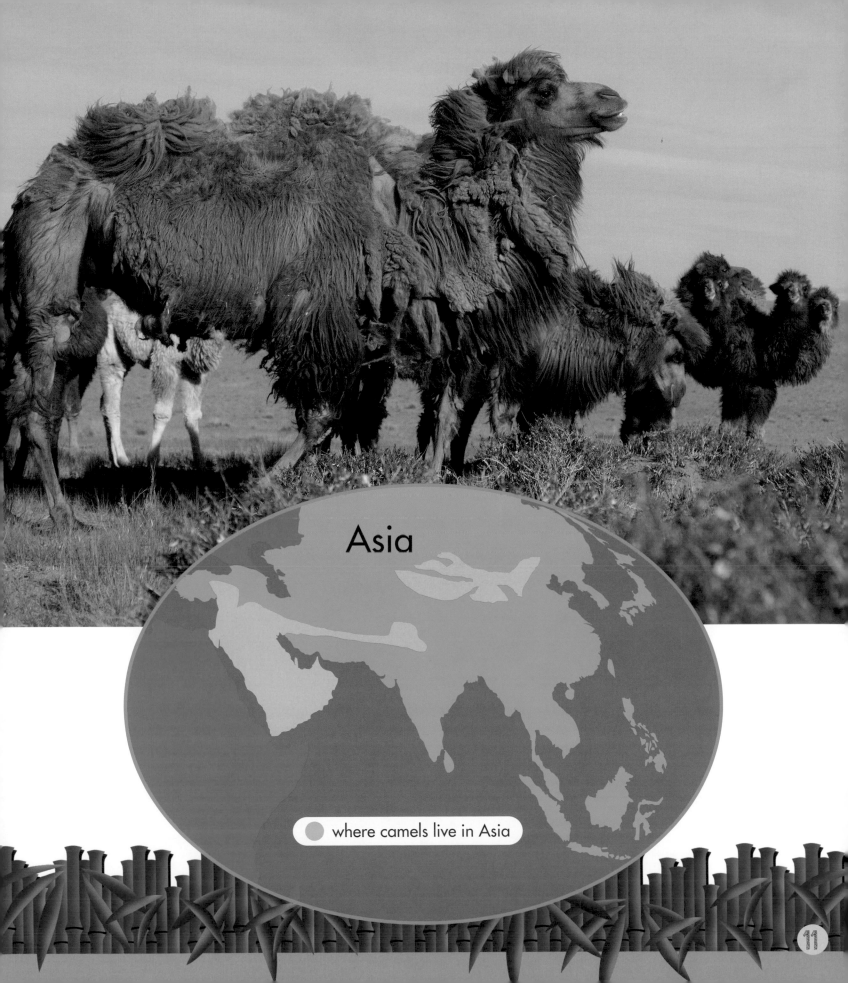

Asia

where camels live in Asia

Life in the Desert

Camels have features that help them live in hot, sandy deserts. Thick eyelashes shade their eyes from the blazing sun. They can close their nostrils to keep out blowing sand.

Wink! You have two eyelids. A camel has three. A camel's extra eyelid blinks sideways to protect its eyes from sand.

Deserts can be very hot during the day.
But they can be cold at night. **Brrrrr!**
Bactrian camels have thick, woolly coats
to keep them warm.

When a camel takes a step, its toes spread out. Skin between its toes keeps the camel's feet from sinking into the soft sand.

A Tough Bite

Camels are herbivores. They eat plants. But most desert plants have sharp spines and pointy thorns. **Ouch!**

Luckily a camel's upper lip is split.
A camel can move each part of its lip
separately. Camels use their upper
lips like fingers to eat prickly food.

Bulls, Cows, and Calves

An adult male camel is called a bull. In about the middle of winter, bulls start to get noisy. And stinky too! They grunt and roar. They even foam at the mouth.

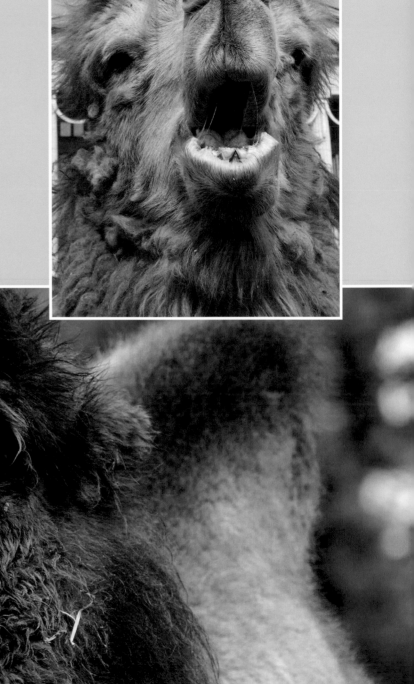

Bulls get smelly and act tough to attract mates. Female camels are called cows. After mating, the bull wanders off to be with other males. The pregnant cows gather together.

A pregnant cow gives birth to a calf after 13 to 15 months. Females usually have one calf at a time.

A newborn calf is about the size of a large dog. Less than an hour after birth, it can stand, walk, and even run.

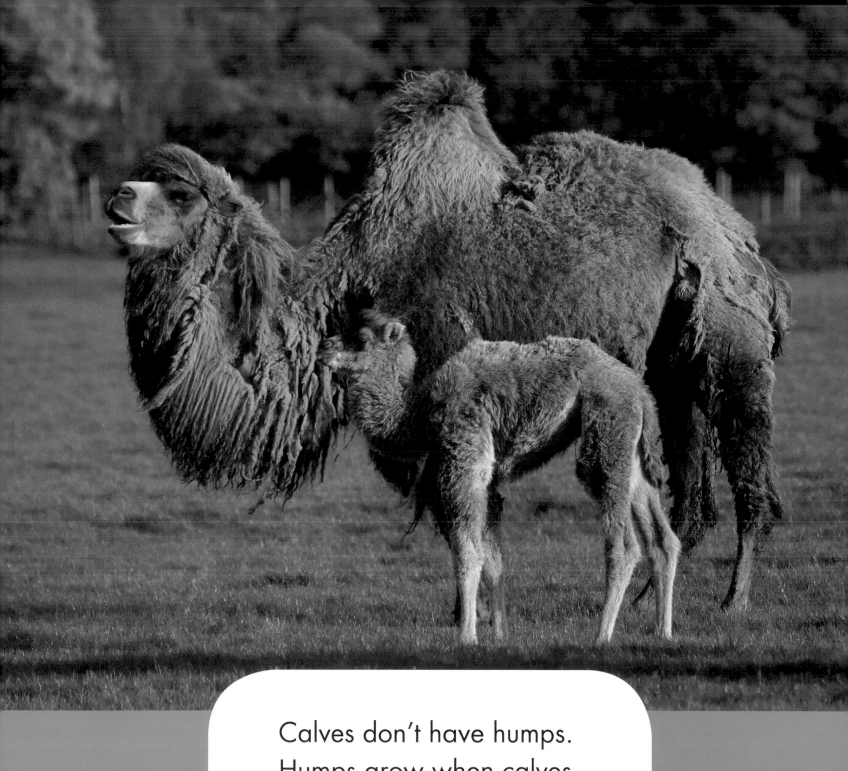

Calves don't have humps. Humps grow when calves start to eat plants instead of their mother's milk. Calves stay with their mothers for about two years.

Big Desert Animals

Many desert animals, such as snakes and lizards, are small. They cannot harm a camel. Adult camels are even too big for mighty lions to easily kill. A pack of wolves may chase down a wild camel. But most predators just leave camels alone. Healthy camels can live up to 50 years.

The biggest danger to wild camels is people. People pollute the places where camels live. They let goats graze in places camels search for food. Some people even kill camels for their meat.

Fewer than 1,000 Bactrian camels live in the wild. One day these camels could become extinct.

Camels Are Awesome

Today some people in Asia race camels. Camels can run up to 40 miles (64 kilometers) per hour. That's as fast as a horse!

Camels are awesome. They can survive in harsh deserts. And people could never have crossed dry, sandy deserts without them.

Glossary

Bactrian (BAK-tre-uhn)—a type of camel that has two humps

dromedary—(DROHM-ah-dayr-ee)—a type of camel that has one hump

energy (EN-uhr-jee)—the strength to do activities without getting tired

extinct (ik-STINKT)—no longer living; an extinct animal is one that has died out, with no more of its kind

graze (GRAYZ)—to eat grass and other plants

herbivore (HUR-buh-vor)—an animal that eats only plants

mate (MATE)—to join together to produce young

pollute (puh-LOOT)—to make something dirty or unsafe

predator (PRED-uh-tur)—an animal that hunts other animals for food

pregnant (PREG-nuhnt)—carrying unborn young within the body; a pregnant female camel has one calf at a time

tame (TAME)—trained to live with or be useful to people

Read More

Ganeri, Anita. *Bactrian Camel.* A Day in the Life. Chicago: Heinemann Library, 2011.

Goldish, Meish. *Camel.* Desert Animals: Searchin' for Shade. New York: Bearport Publishing, 2015.

Gray, Susan H. *Camels Have Humps.* Tell Me Why? Ann Arbor, Mich.: Cherry Lake Publishing, 2015.

Internet Sites

FactHound offers a safe, fun way to find Internet sites related to this book. All of the sites on FactHound have been researched by our staff.

Here's all you do:
Visit *www.facthound.com*
Type in this code: 9781491439043

 Super-cool stuff!

Check out projects, games and lots more at
www.capstonekids.com

Critical Thinking Using the Common Core

1. Look at the photo on page 6. Is this a dromedary or Bactrian camel? How do you know? (Integration of Knowledge and Ideas)

2. How does a camel's hump help it travel long distances? (Key Ideas and Details)

3. One day Bactrian camels may become extinct. What does "extinct" mean? (Craft and Structure)

Index